A LOOK AT US HISTORY

THE FRENCH AND INDIAN WAR

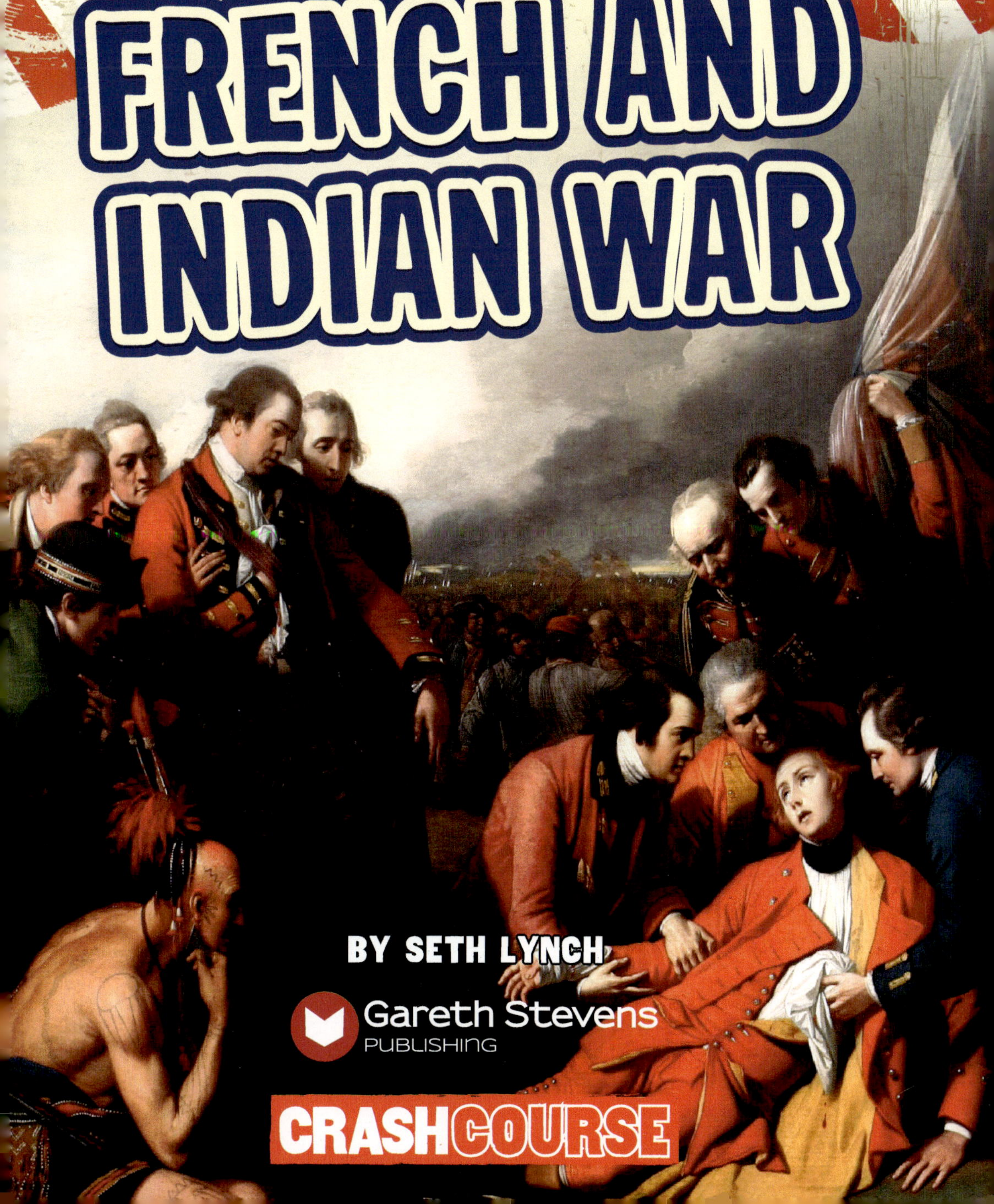

BY SETH LYNCH

Gareth Stevens PUBLISHING

CRASHCOURSE

Please visit our website, www.garethstevens.com. For a free color catalog of all our high-quality books, call toll free 1-800-542-2595 or fax 1-877-542-2596.

Library of Congress Cataloging-in-Publication Data

Names: Lynch, Seth, author.
Title: The French and Indian War / Seth Lynch.
Description: New York : Gareth Stevens Publishing, 2019. | Series: A look at US history | Includes index.
Identifiers: LCCN 2017050822| ISBN 9781538221235 (library bound) | ISBN 9781538221259 (pbk.) | ISBN 9781538221266 (6 pack)
Subjects: LCSH: United States--History--French and Indian War, 1754-1763--Juvenile literature.
Classification: LCC E199 .L96 2018 | DDC 973.2/6--dc23 LC record available at https://lccn.loc.gov/2017050822

First Edition

Published in 2019 by
Gareth Stevens Publishing
111 East 14th Street, Suite 349
New York, NY 10003

Designer: Samantha DeMartin
Editor: Kristen Nelson

Photo credits: Series art Christophe BOISSON/Shutterstock.com; (feather quill) Galushko Sergey/Shutterstock.com; (parchment) mollicart-design/Shutterstock.com; cover, p. 1 Themadchopper/Wikimedia Commons; p. 5 Leemage/Universal Images Group/Getty Images; p. 7 Bardocz Peter/Shutterstock.com; p. 9 Scewing/Wikimedia Commons; p. 11 Culture Club/Hulton Archive/Getty Images; p. 13 PhotoQuest/Archive Photos/Getty Images; p. 15 adoc-photos/Corbis Historical/Getty Images; p. 17 Stock Montage/Archive Photos/Getty Images; pp. 19, 23 Hulton Archive/Hulton Archive/Getty Images; p. 21 Print Collector/Hulton Archive/Getty Images; p. 25 Archive Photos/Archive Photos/Getty Images; p. 27 Universal History Archive/Universal Images Group Editorial/Getty Images; p. 29 H. Armstrong Roberts/ClassicStock/Getty Images.

Printed in the United States of America

CPSIA compliance information: Batch #CS18GS: For further information contact Gareth Stevens, New York, New York at 1-800-542-2595.

CONTENTS

Words in the glossary appear in **bold** type the first time they are used in the text.

CLAIMING THE LAND

Big parts of North America had been claimed by Great Britain, France, and Spain by the mid-1700s. They all wanted to keep these claims and gain even more land. Soon, **tensions** over these land claims **erupted** into what's now called the French and Indian War.

MAKE THE GRADE

When Europeans claimed land for their country, they were claiming areas that had often belonged to Native Americans for thousands of years.

Great Britain had settled 13 colonies along the East Coast. New France included part of Canada and lands found along the Mississippi River as far south as Louisiana. The two countries disagreed about the borders of these lands, especially near Lake Ontario and the Ohio River.

MAKE THE GRADE

Spain claimed Florida in the 1500s and also had claims to present-day Texas, California, New Mexico, and Mexico.

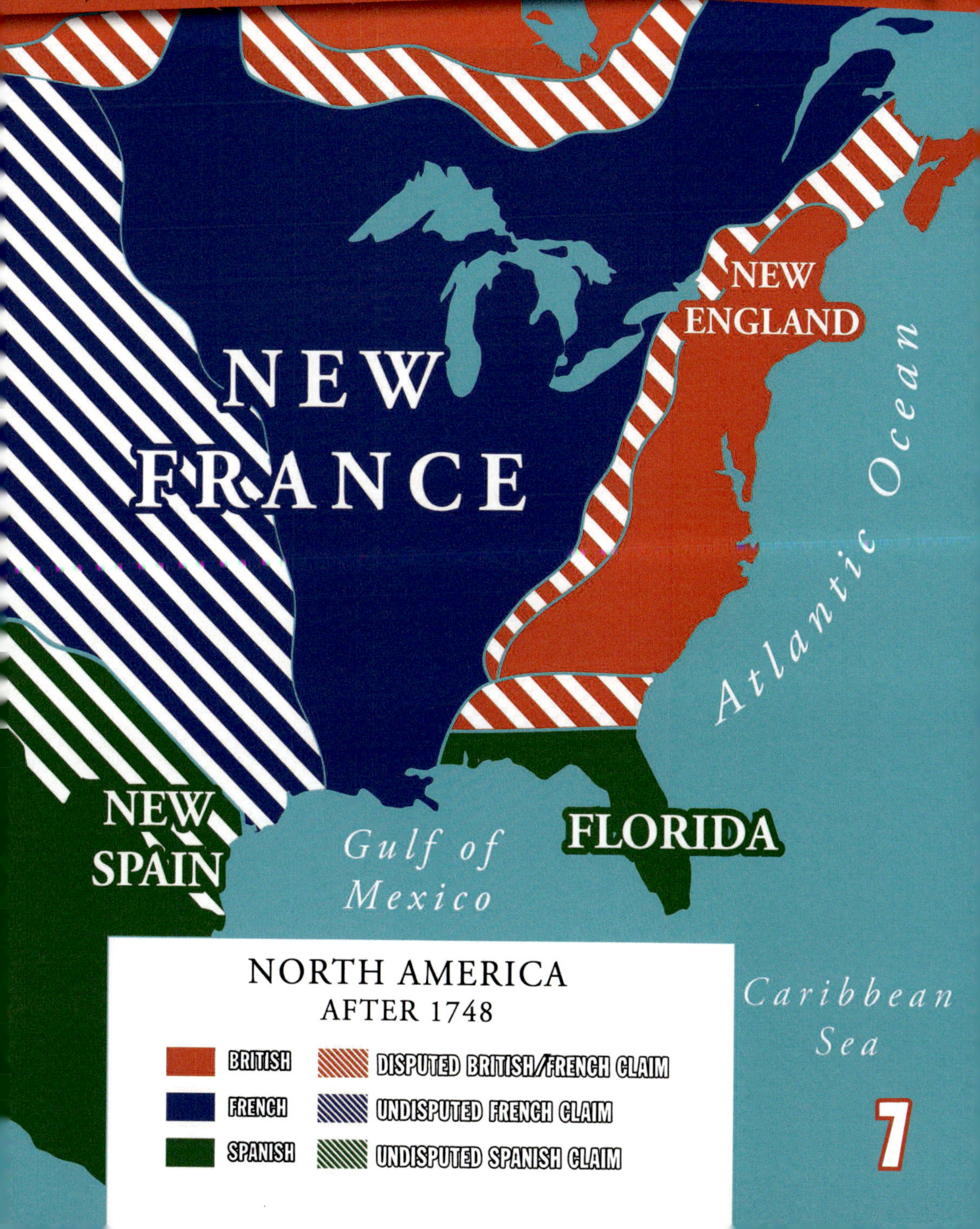

TENSION MOUNTS

During the 1750s, British colonists were moving onto land claimed by the French. By 1754, France had started building a fort in present-day Pennsylvania on land the British felt they also had claimed. French forces also captured British settlements in the area.

MAKE THE GRADE

The British sent 21-year-old George Washington and a party of other men to force the French off British land. The French refused to go, claiming the land was theirs.

BATTLE BEGINS

The French called their new fort Fort Duquesne (doo-KAYN). British forces, including Washington, were sent out to **demand** the French give back the land. In May 1754, French and British forces met in the Battle of Jumonville Glen.

MAKE THE GRADE

In July 1754, Washington had to surrender, or give up, at the Battle of Fort Necessity. Because of this loss, General Edward Braddock was sent to the colonies to lead the British forces in North America. He died in battle in 1755.

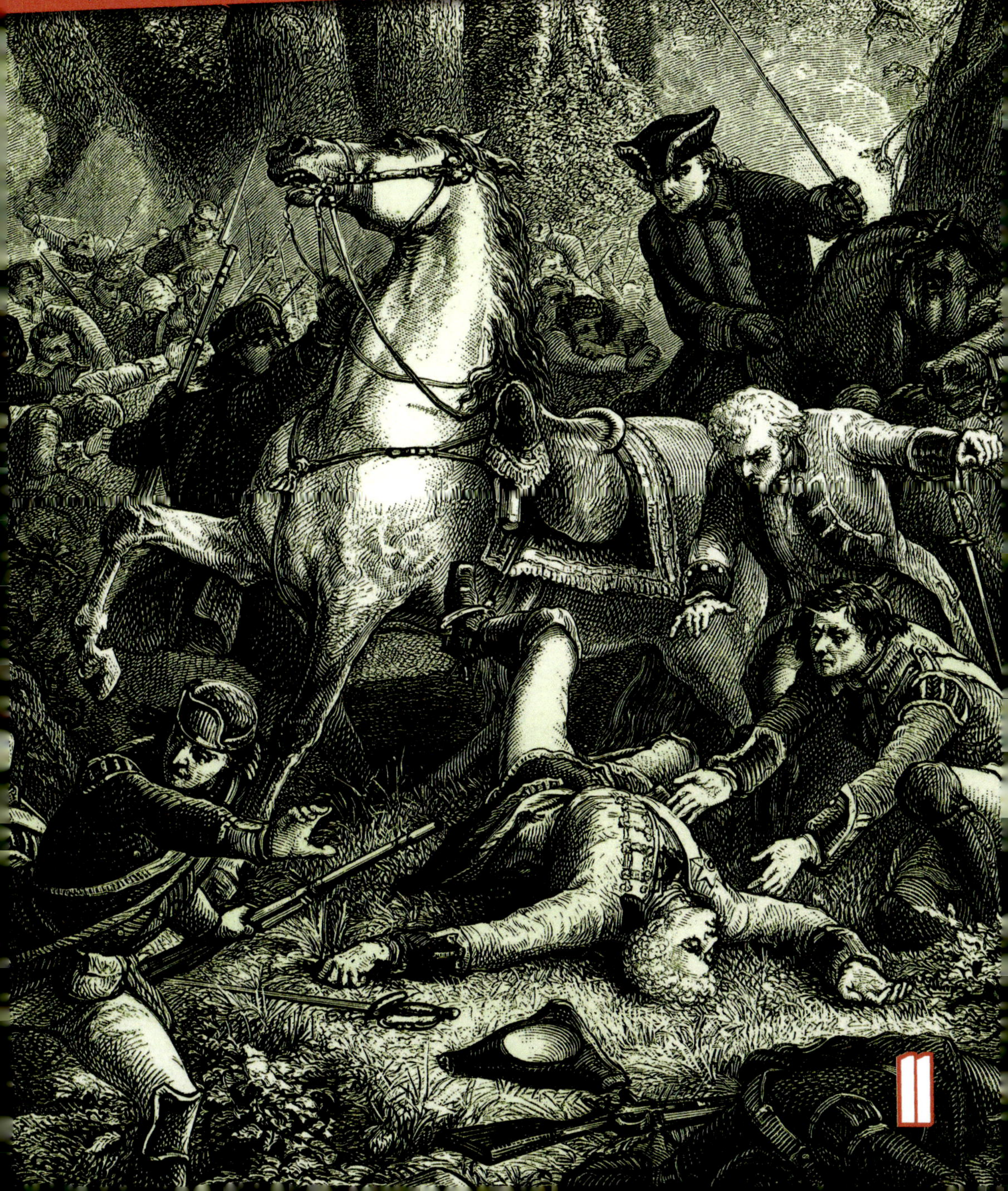

TAKING SIDES

The Native American groups living in the Ohio River valley, where much of the war took place, fought on both sides, though more fought for the French. The Iroquois Confederacy, a large and powerful group in New York, fought with the British.

MAKE THE GRADE

Historians gave the war its name because of the many Native Americans who took part. They wanted control of their own land and likely fought on the side they thought would give them the best deal after the war.

THE LARGER WAR

The French and Indian War was the North American part of a larger war. The European part of the war began in 1756 over Austria trying to reclaim land in Europe. Today it's called the Seven Years' War. At first, France had many successes.

MAKE THE GRADE

Great Britain and France also fought over colonial claims in India during the Seven Years' War.

While the Seven Years' War raged in Europe and elsewhere, the **conflict** in North America slowed for a time. By the late 1750s, the British forces started to claim more victories. In 1759, the British took Fort Carillon, found at the end of Lake Champlain.

MAKE THE GRADE

The British changed the name of Fort Carillon to Fort Ticonderoga.

CANADIAN INVASION

Later that year, the British **invaded** Canada, starting with Quebec. Quebec was built at a part of the St. Lawrence River that allowed entry into the rest of New France. After a battle, the French surrendered the city, giving the British control of Canada.

MAKE THE GRADE

Built on a cliff overlooking the river, Quebec had some natural **protection**.

In 1760, British forces took Montreal, too. The capture of Montreal was the end of the fighting in North America in the French and Indian War. Still, fighting between the **allies** of Great Britain and the allies of France continued abroad.

MAKE THE GRADE

It's important to remember that many other European countries took part in the Seven Years' War. North America was most affected by the conflicts between Great Britain and France along with Spain.

SPAIN JOINS FRANCE

In 1762, Spain joined France against the British. Their agreement was called the Family Compact, since the king of France and king of Spain were cousins. It made little difference. Many losses and events in Europe led France to seek peace in 1762.

MAKE THE GRADE

Spain's ships were no match for the powerful British navy, which took the French Caribbean Islands, the Philippines, and Spanish Cuba.

THE TREATY

The Seven Years' War and French and Indian War officially ended with the signing of the **Treaty** of Paris in 1763. Great Britain formally took **possession** of French Canada as well as France's land east of the Mississippi River and in India, Africa, and the Mediterranean.

MAKE THE GRADE

France had tried to start peace talks years earlier, but the British government offered terms they couldn't accept.

Spain gained French land west of the Mississippi. Even though Great Britain won Cuba in the war, the treaty returned it to Spain. However, Florida was added to British territory in North America. France regained the islands it lost to Great Britain in the Caribbean.

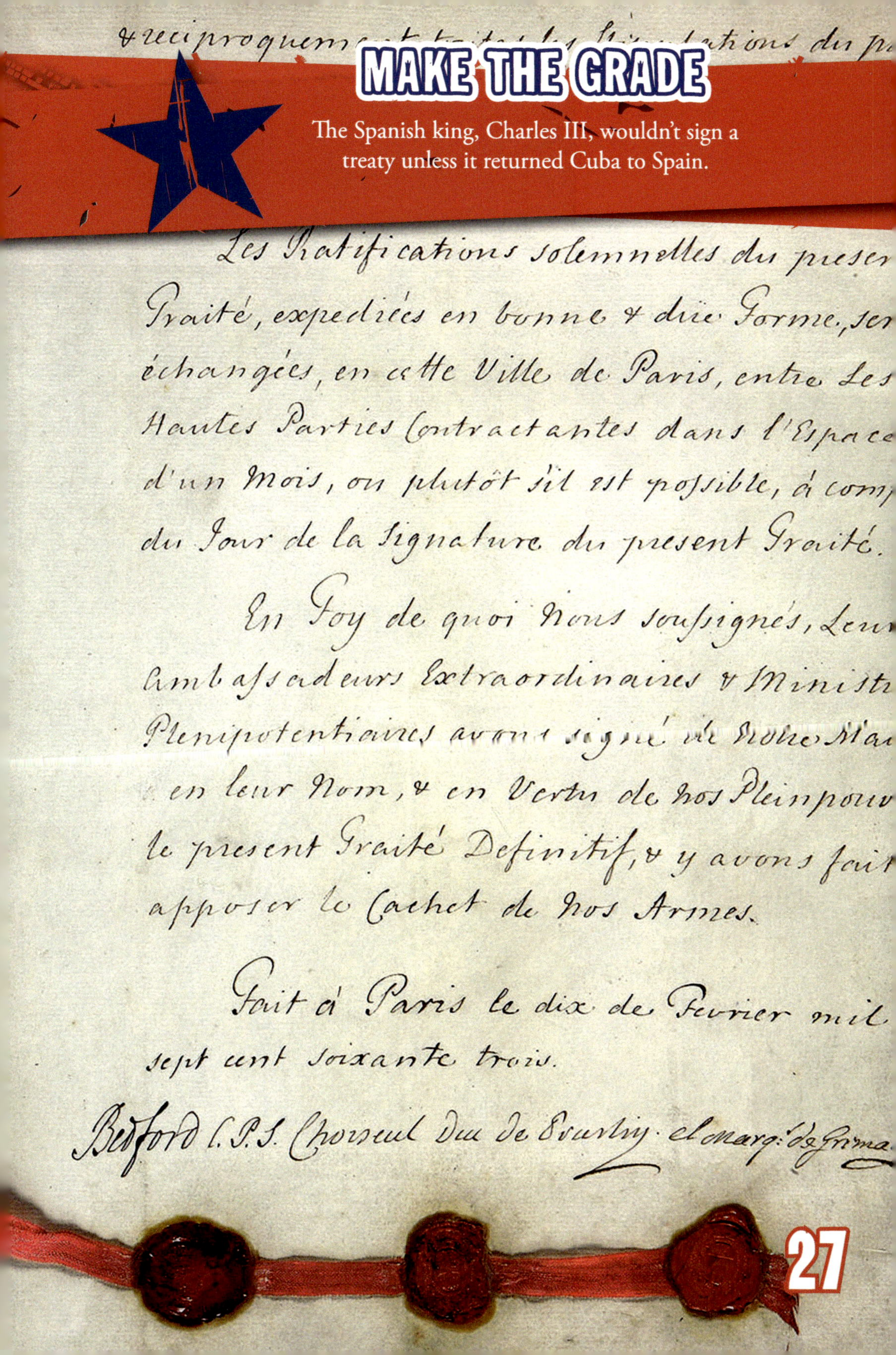
& reciproquement toutes les Stipulations du p

Les Ratifications solemnelles du preser
Traité, expediées en bonne & due Forme, ser
échangées, en cette Ville de Paris, entre Les
Hautes Parties Contractantes dans l'Espace
d'un Mois, ou plutôt s'il est possible, à com
du Jour de la Signature du present Traité.

En Foy de quoi Nous soussignés, Leur
Ambassadeurs Extraordinaires & Ministr
Plenipotentiaires avons signé de notre Mai
en leur Nom, & en Vertu de nos Pleinpouv
le present Traité Definitif, & y avons fait
apposer le Cachet de nos Armes.

Fait à Paris le dix de Fevrier mil
sept cent soixante trois.

Bedford C.P.S. Choiseul Duc de Praslin. el marq: de Grima

MAKE THE GRADE

The Spanish king, Charles III, wouldn't sign a treaty unless it returned Cuba to Spain.

WAR, A CAUSE FOR WAR

The war put Great Britain in **debt**. They passed laws taxing the North American colonists and didn't allow the colonists to settle in the newly claimed lands. This angered the British colonists. These were two causes of the American Revolution, which began in 1775.

MAKE THE GRADE

As Great Britain took control of Ohio, Native Americans there worried about colonists moving onto their land. Some tried to force the British colonists out in Pontiac's Rebellion.

TIMELINE OF THE FRENCH AND INDIAN WAR

1750s
Borders between French and British lands in North America are unclear. They cause tension.

1754
The French build a fort on land the British also claim. The British lose the Battle of Fort Necessity.

1756
The Seven Years' War begins in Europe.

1759
British forces invade Canada and take Fort Carillon and then Quebec.

1760
Great Britain captures Montreal. Fighting ends in North America.

1762
Spain joins France in fighting the British in the Family Compact.

1763
The Treaty of Paris ends the war.

GLOSSARY

ally: one of two or more people or groups who work together

conflict: a disagreement or fight

debt: the state of owing money

demand: to forcefully state that someone must give you something

erupt: to burst forth

invade: to enter a place to take it over

possession: ownership

protection: the act of keeping safe from harm

tension: a state of anger between groups

treaty: an agreement between countries

FOR MORE INFORMATION

Books

Caravantes, Peggy. *The French and Indian War*. Minneapolis, MN: ABDO Publishing Company, 2013.

Gagne, Tammy. *The French and Indian War*. Hallandale, FL: Mitchell Lane Publishers, 2017.

Website

The War That Made America

www.pbs.org/thewarthatmadeamerica/timeline.html

Check out this timeline to review what you've learned about the French and Indian War.

Publisher's note to educators and parents: Our editors have carefully reviewed this website to ensure that they are suitable for students. Many websites change frequently, however, and we cannot guarantee that a site's future contents will continue to meet our high standards of quality and educational value. Be advised that students should be closely supervised whenever they access the internet.

INDEX